An Awesome Way to PRAY
JOURNAL

"Mobilizing Students for Powerful Prayer"

Barry St. Clair

LIFEWAY PRESS
NASHVILLE, TENNESSEE

ISBN 0-7673-9086-5

Dewey Decimal Classification: 248.3
Subject Heading: PRAYER / YOUTH—RELIGIOUS LIFE

Unless otherwise indicated, biblical quotations are from :
The Holy Bible, *New International Version,* copyright ©
1973, 1978, 1984 by International Bible Society. Used by
permission.

Scripture quotations identified as KJV are taken from the
King James Version of the Bible.

Scripture quotations identified as CEV are taken from the
Contemporary English Version. Copyright © 1991, 1992, 1995
American Bible Society. Used by permission.

Scripture quotations identified as TEV are from the *Today's
English Version, Second Edition.* Copyright © 1966, 1971,
1976, 1992. American Bible Society. Used by permission.

Printed in the United States of America

LifeWay Press
127 Ninth Avenue, North
Nashville, Tennessee 37234

About the Writer

Dr. Barry St. Clair is executive director of Reach Out Youth Solutions Barry equips youth leaders, students, and parents worldwide to become fully devoted followers of Christ. Dr. St. Clair has served as director of youth evangelism for the Southern Baptist Convention, co-founder of the National Network of Youth Ministries, and a leader of the "See You at the Pole" prayer event. He has written over 20 books.

Reach Out Youth Solutions seeks to see as many teenagers as possible become fully devoted followers of Christ. This vision is accomplished by equipping leaders of youth around the world for strategic ministry through the church. Our staff has 30 members located in five countries. Contact Reach Out Youth Solutions at 770-441-2247 for more information.

Thanks

This project became a reality through many people's efforts: Greg Johnson, Brad Leeper, Dave Ronne, Bert Ross, Steve Young, Susan Nichols, Jason Ricks, Jeff Keech, Sharon Stanton, and Rick A. Mills.

Barry St. Clair

Dedication

This book is dedicated to **Greg Simmons,** 1947-1988, my prayer partner and friend. He was a successful business-man, youth leader, creative genius, committed son, husband, father of five, and a lover of God.

As college students, Greg and I disciplined ourselves to pray together every morning. Out of our praying together, the Fellowship of Christian Athletes began on our campus as a significant ministry to high school students where many young people accepted Christ.

Really, this is where *An Awesome Way to Pray* was born—praying with Greg Simmons. My hope is that our prayer and evangelism legacy will multiply to millions of students who are just like we were.

Barry St. Clair

Hi!

My name is Becky. I'm in the fifth week of *An Awesome Way to Pray*, but about two and a half weeks ago God started challenging me about this whole "Love" thing. So what is "loving your friends"? Loving your friends is loving God. I've noticed that a lot of my friendships are surface friendships, leaving me dissatisfied and wondering why. The truth is there is still some junk deep down inside of me, junk that I want to replace with God's love. I know that I can never love God as much as He loves me, but I want to always be making more room for His love. *An Awesome Way to Pray* marks a turning point for me. It's a covenant I've made to invest the love God has for me into my friends.

Greetings!

Our youth group has been participating in *An Awesome Way to Pray*. It's a movement of God in our youth group. For the past three weeks we've been focusing on being broken for our friends. That's hard work! It's easy to get wrapped up in your own life and think that nothing you could say could possibly make a difference in another person's life. Also some situations and individuals look hopeless. God has revealed to me that when I trust Him with all of my heart something of value can happen through me!

Hello!

My name is Jon and I'm a 10th grade student. Before I owned my faith and before I genuinely cared about my friends, church was something I seldom talked about. When something "spiritual" did come up, I either ignored or shrugged it off. I felt uncomfortable talking about spiritual matters with my friends. In the past few months, God has changed how I view and act toward my friends. Instead of dreading the mention of church, I've felt disappointment over lost opportunities. I've developed a love for my friends. I have prayed and sought out opportunities to witness to my friends. Through my youth pastor, *An Awesome Way to Pray*, and God's voice, I've begun to learn how to communicate with my friends and how to share my faith.

Contents

Introduction

An Awesome Way to PRAY JOURNAL

3 Christian Students
Meeting 3 Times a Week to Pray for
3 Non-Christian Friends

What's the Big Deal About Doing This?

Over the next 30 days it will empower you:

To grow in your intimacy with God;
To encourage you between your youth group meetings;
To equip you to make a powerful spiritual impact on your friends' lives.
To show you how God can use you to make a difference at your school.

So What Is This "An Awesome Way to Pray" Stuff Anyway?

God is at work on campuses all across the world! "See You at the Pole," for instance, has become a worldwide event. From humble beginnings in Texas just a few years ago with a handful of kids, it has grown to the extent that literally millions of students around the world participated last year. It has been characterized as "the biggest prayer meeting in history," and for once the hype is true. Movements like "True Love Waits" and the growth of Christian clubs are sweeping the nation.

The logical questions we should ask are: "Great, is following Jesus just big events?" or "Can I do something every day to make a difference?" Out of those questions was born An Awesome Way to Pray. An Awesome Way to Pray is designed to move you from events to a daily process—in other words, taking your faith from the big event to a daily passion.

If your group is participating in "An Awesome Way to Pray," you and two of your friends will commit to pray not only for your school, but also for three specific friends who do not know Jesus Christ. And, along with praying, you'll begin to look for ways to communicate Jesus Christ to them.

In a nutshell, it's:

Three Christian friends,
Meeting three times a week to pray,
For three friends who need Christ.

Important! Even if your youth group isn't "formally" participating in "An Awesome Way to Pray," you can still meet with two of your friends, three times a week, praying for three friends who need Christ. Encourage them to get this book, *An Awesome Way to Pray*, and study it along with you.

Rocking Your Socks

God wants to use you! Amazing ! You have a great opportunity on your campus to make a difference. If you and two others join together to do this, then you and your friends will be prepared to see God sweep across your friends lives, your school, and eventually your nation. *An Awesome Way to Pray* is designed to help you make a difference!

An Awesome Way to Pray is flexible and practical. Here are ways you can max it out:

• As a guide to take you deeper into your walk with Christ.

- As a way you and two of your friends can develop a prayer strategy to impact your non-Christian friends and your campus.

- As a journal to help you keep track of what God is doing in your life.

Realistically, it will challenge your socks off!

You'll pray more than you've ever prayed before. Some of your friends will become interested in Jesus and what it means to follow Him. And they will look to you for some answers. Are you ready? Some people will laugh at you and reject you. People have gotten killed doing this stuff.

A 14-year-old freshman turned a gun on a prayer group at Heath High School in West Paducah, Kentucky, killing three girls and wounding five others. Through that tragedy hundreds of students have come to Christ. Now 200-300 students come to that prayer meeting every week. You've got to decide if you are willing to pay the price—even if it costs you your life!

By using this book, you can count on these positive results:

- If you've had an inconsistent prayer life, then you can experience God in powerful prayer!

- If you've been afraid, then you can beat the fear barrier in sharing your faith.

- If you've been praying for some of your non-Christian friends, then some will begin considering the claims of Jesus Christ.

• If some of your friends are not Christians, then some of your friends may come to faith in Christ!

Take the Prayer Power Challenge

The challenge has two parts.

1. Spending time alone with God every day for six weeks.

2. Praying with your friends three times a week for the next six weeks.

The only reason the challenge lasts only six weeks is to get you in the habit of meeting with God and your friends. The goal is to do these things all year long.

Ready to make this six week commitment? Decide now to go for it, but don't commit on the basis of your emotions. Determine that you'll follow through even on the days when you don't feel like it. When you do, God is going to work in and through you—big time.

If you're ready to commit, write your name below:

_____

Jump Start

To get you off to a great start, here are some ways you can get the most out of using this book every day.

For Your Daily Time with God:

Choose a time.
It's important to set a specific time to meet the Lord each day. Jesus often spent time with His Father in the morn-

ings, and His is a great example to follow *(Mark 1:25)*. Have you ever seen a football team warm up after the game? Or a band warm up after a concert? No. In the same way, God wants you to warm up with Him as your day begins. All the excuses of "I'm not a morning person" aside, it just makes more sense to start the day with Him.

Faithfully meet with God every day at the time you choose. You may know what it feels like to be stood up on a date or to plan to meet someone who doesn't show up. God understands and forgives your weaknesses, but He still wants you to make and keep your appointment with Him.

Remember: God wants to spend time with you. Write the time you want to meet with God daily: _____

Choose a place.
It's usually much easier to communicate with God if you can be alone with Him in a place where you won't be distracted. Abraham talked to God in the desert, Moses on the mountain top, and Daniel in his room.

Think of a good place to meet with the Lord, and write it here: _____

Choose to prepare.
As you begin your time alone with God, your mental attitude is critical. Don't set your alarm for 30 seconds before you are supposed to meet with the Lord, or you're likely to have a "time asleep with God." Get up, shower, and get dressed.

Write the physical barriers that can keep you from being prepared to meet with God:

Now, count on God to meet you. You're in for some exciting surprises!

For Your Prayer Power Team:

If you want to make a difference in your friends' lives, here's how: Spend some time this week evaluating your relationships. Answer these questions:

What two Christian friends can I partner with to pray?

Write their names here:

1. _____

2. _____

Who are three non-Christian friends my two Christian friends and I are concerned about and would like to pray for?

Write their names here:

1. _____

2. _____

3. _____

Write when and where we will be praying for them this week?

1. _____

2. _____

3. _____

When you pray with your friends you have all kinds of options. Some things you need to do every time you meet:

• Commit with your two friends to do these devotionals by yourselves during the week.

• When you meet together, spend one-third of your time sharing what God has taught you through your quiet time and the other two-thirds of your time praying for each other and your non-Christian friends.

• Begin praying immediately. Don't spend half of your time talking about your prayer requests.

• Pray for each other. Be open and honest about your needs. Share them with each other in prayer.

• Pray for your friends who need Christ. Pray for their specific needs.

• Ask God to show you how to love your lost friends and how to share the love of Jesus with them.

• If you run into spiritual issues or problems with non-Christian friends or others at school that are too big to handle, then read and apply 2 *Corinthians 10:4-5.* Then talk to your youth leader about it.

You can use these creative options too:

- Do a prayer walk around your school.

- Conduct a concert of prayer with all the students who are in prayer teams.

- Try praying through your school yearbook.

- Pray locker-to-locker for every person in your school.

- Go room-to-room asking God to work in the lives of students and teachers in every room in your school.

- Take prayer requests from people at school, asking what you can pray for them.

- Stand at the doorway of your school and pray for every person who comes in the door.

The list is as long as you are creative! Go for it!

Maxing It Out

To keep motivated to continue every day, follow these suggestions for your time with God and your prayer team:

- **Go to bed on time.**
Pass on the Letterman Top 10 and go to bed at a decent hour. You can't go to bed late and expect to wake up fresh the next morning. You can't expect spiritual peace if you're a physical wreck.

- **Get up in the morning.**
You probably don't bounce up out of bed with enthusiastic, "Good Morning, Lord!" Most of us would rather smash the alarm clock with a hammer and go back to sleep. There's no magic solution. When the alarm sounds, throw your feet

out of the bed, plant them on the floor, and stand up. Don't rationalize. Just get up.

• Look to Jesus.
Don't start the day worrying about the bad things that might happen. Let your first conscious thoughts in the morning focus on Jesus Christ. Ask Him how He wants to use you today.

• Don't give up.
If you miss your time alone with God one morning, or your time with your prayer team, don't worry about it and beat yourself up. You wouldn't quit eating if you missed a meal! You aren't a failure. Just try your best not to miss the next time.

• Be honest.
If it feels like your time alone with God is empty and worthless, or your prayer team is dead, tell God about it. But don't quit. He'd much rather have your honest complaints than your absence.

• Be consistent.
Some of your times alone with God, and your prayer times with your team, will be wonderful. Others will just be routine. But the way you feel is not always an accurate indicator of success. Every day that you pray will help you grow stronger, even if you don't sense the results right away.

• Use the journal.
Write down what you are learning in your time with God and in your prayer team. You'll be amazed at how you look back and see how God has worked in your life.

What You See/What You Get

So you will know what you are doing, check out one of the pages. This is what you'll see on the left page.

The Big Idea.
This devotional thought for the day will include a short Scripture passage.

Think About It.
A simple summary will help you get the Scripture clearly in your mind as you read it several times.

What's the Point?
This suggested "ACTION POINT" will move you from a time of prayer and reflection to taking a positive and specific action.

Prayer.
This guided prayer will help you connect with the Lord and focus on the day.

The right page works like this:

Quote.
An inspirational quote to encourage and challenge you.

Journal.
Use this section to:
- Write out your prayers.
- Reflect on what you think God is showing you.
- Record what happened yesterday.
- Write things you need to do today.
- Record answers to prayers from your prayer team.

Today's Action.

Look up and read the Scripture verses indicated in this section. Spend time alone with God and meditate on what the verse means. Then,—this is important!—write one specific action you will take that will allow God to use you. Hopefully this will come out of your time alone with God.

Continue this every day for six weeks, then ask God what He wants to do from there.

An Awesome Way to PRAY

JOURNAL

3 Christian Students
Meeting 3 Times a Week to Pray for
3 Non-Christian Friends

Weeks 1 – 6

Something Bigger

The Big Idea

There's a big difference in going to a sporting event and watching one on TV. There's something about being caught up in the noise and excitement of a crowd you can't capture sitting on your couch. You just get swept up in the passion and fun of the game. See You at the Pole and True Love Waits are those kinds of events. Literally millions of students around the world have participated in them.

Perhaps you know what it's like to take a stand with a group of your friends...and the thrill of knowing that, around the world, you don't stand alone.

So, what's next? You've got to move beyond the big event to developing a lifestyle that pleases God. Easy? No. Scary? You bet. Worthwhile and rewarding? Absolutely!

> *After they prayed, the place where they were meeting was shaken. And they were all filled with the Holy Spirit and spoke the word of God boldly* (Acts 4:31).

What's the Point?

Obviously, there's something miraculous about prayer. Here's the point: You want your lifestyle to change to reflect what God is doing in your life. The critical element of that change is prayer. Are you ready for the next level?

Think About It

God is at work all around you. He wants you to be part of something bigger than yourself.

Prayer

Lord, I sure would like to be able to see the world and my friends through Your eyes. Give me that kind of sight, and give me the courage to do something about what I see.

> You can impress people at a distance. But you can impact them only up close.[1] —Unknown

JOURNAL
(QUIET TIME NOTES, PRAYER NEEDS, TODAY'S TO-DO'S)

Today's Action

Read *John 4:35.* In your prayer partnerships, keep your eyes and your heart open to the spiritual needs of your friends. Realize that this is the first step in God's process of using you to reach your non-Christian friends.

Therefore, I need to. . .

Being a Friend at All Times

The Big Idea
You're the product of a lot of people—parents, grand-parents, great-grandparents, and so on all make up your family tree.

As a Christian, you can see a process at work the day God brought you to Himself. Just as your personality is made of many different people, God used many people and circumstances to help you realize you needed Jesus.

> The first thing Andrew did was find his own brother Simon and tell him "We have found the Messiah" (that is, Christ). And he brought him to Jesus (John 1:41-42).

After meeting Jesus, Andrew went right to his brother and introduced him to his new Master. There's a principle here: It takes a friend to bring a friend to Jesus. If you look at your own relationship with Christ, chances are many people had a hand in bringing you to Him. Some may have been praying for you, others taking you to church or youth group meetings, and some may have verbally shared with you. And God used all these tools to call you to Himself.

What's the Point?
You're God's tool to reach others. That's His intent for each of us. Pray, be available, and watch what happens.

Think About It
You are a crucial part of what God wants to do in reaching non-Christian students. You're not necessarily the only part, but you sure have an important role to play.

Prayer
Father, thank You so much for all of those who played a part in bringing me to You. Help me to be that same kind of person for someone else.

Some things do not change. If God ever loved me, He loves me now. That is what unchangeable means. If ever God forgave me, He forgives me now...If God ever saved me, He saved me forever.[2]
—Dan DeHann

JOURNAL
(QUIET TIME NOTES, PRAYER NEEDS, TODAY'S TO-DO'S)

| |
| |
| |
| |
| |
| |
| |
| |

Today's Action

Read *Acts 8:34-35*. Talk with your prayer partners about the circumstances that brought you to Christ. Thank God for all those who played a part in your becoming a Christian.

Therefore, I need to. . .

The Pressure's Off

The Big Idea

Relax. You're off the hook. You can't "save" anyone. Nor can anyone else. God is in the salvation business. He is the only One who can redeem non-Christians. After all, He is God.

> *The Spirit will show them that they are wrong about sin, because they didn't have faith in Me* (John 16:9, CEV).

It is God's Spirit who leads us to see we're sinners. We might have convincing arguments, but apart from God it's all just words anyway.

So, what's your responsibility in God's plan? After all, God will save whomever He wants, whenever He wants. Are you excused from doing anything? Nope. Yesterday we talked about the chain of events and people that led you to Christ. The person that told you about Jesus was sensitive enough and faithful enough to tell you about Jesus.

What's the Point?

So, even if you're off the hook when it comes to the results, you aren't off the hook when it comes to obedience. It's not a matter of you charging off to the first non-Christian in sight. It's simply drawing close to God in prayer. As He leads, you communicate Christ to your friends. Salvation isn't your responsibility, but faithfulness is.

Think About It

You can't save anyone. God saves people, but He expects us to be faithful and obedient as He leads us.

Prayer

Father, I'm so thankful that You trust me enough to give me the opportunity to share You with my friends. Help me to be faithful, obedient, and pleasing to You.

Today, this moment, He [God] feels toward His creatures, toward babies, toward the sick, the fallen, the sinful, exactly as He did when He sent His only-begotten Son into the world to die for mankind.[3] —A.W. Tozer

JOURNAL
(QUIET TIME NOTES, PRAYER NEEDS, TODAY'S TO-DO'S)

Today's Action

Read *Matthew 19:21-22.* Don't beat yourself up, thinking that you're totally responsible for someone's salvation. How many people did God use to reach you? Talk to your prayer partners about this.

Therefore, I need to. . .

I'll Be There For You

The Big Idea

Talk's cheap. We throw the word *love* around casually. We can say. "I love my mother; I love my dog; I love jelly sandwiches; I love 'X-Files.'" In each case we mean something different. So, how should we express love for our friends?

> *Some friends don't help, but a true friend is closer than your own family* (Prov. 18:24, CEV).

That's a heavy thought. Sort of makes you want to be careful how you treat your pals! Chances are you don't go around telling your friends how much you love them. Beyond telling them, how can you express your love for your friends? One sure method is to pray with them. That's exactly what you're doing with your prayer partners right now. A special bond grows when you pray with someone.

What's the Point?

Probably the ultimate expression of love for another is when you say, "I'll pray for you," and then are faithful to pray. In praying for someone else, you're saying, "You are important to me, and I love you so much, that the best I can do for you is to talk to God about you." You can ask God to bless them, or help them, or most importantly, to bring them to the understanding that they need a Savior.

Think About It

A true friend can be even closer than a family member. If you love your friend, you'll want to pray with them if they're a Christian and pray for them if they're not.

Prayer

Lord, help me to never take for granted the friends You've seen fit to give me.

> There is no lowering of the standard of moral requirement. The Holy One can be compassionate and remain holy because He is God, and not man. Things are possible to Him that are not possible to man.[4] —G. Campbell Morgan

JOURNAL
(QUIET TIME NOTES, PRAYER NEEDS, TODAY'S TO-DO'S)

| |
| |
| |
| |
| |
| |
| |
| |
| |

Today's Action

Read *Romans 12:10*. Continue praying with your prayer partners. As you pray for three non-Christians, ask God to show you how you can express His love for them.

| Therefore, I need to. . . |
| |
| |
| |

Which Risks Will You Take?

The Big Idea

One comedian used to say: "When stepping on the brake, your life is in your foot's hands!" However funny it is, the statement is true. Life is full of risks. We are constantly met with one risk after another. This is the question that we need to ask ourselves: *Which risks are worth it?*

What we need is some sort of measuring stick, or "Risk-O-Meter," that would tell us which risks are worth it and which are not. It all comes down to things that you value.

This week you've begun praying for some friends of yours who aren't Christians. You're praying because you value your friends and want them to be with you in heaven one day. You might hesitate because you also value what people say about you. Which one will you choose? Remember that if you choose to not choose, you are actually choosing to do nothing. Listen to what Joshua said:

> *"Choose for yourselves this day whom you will serve"* (Josh. 24:15).

What's the Point?

Which do you value more—your friends themselves? Or what your friends think about you? Loving your friends is a risky business. But it sure is worth the risk!

Think About It

Loving your friends and praying for them may be risky and even affect what people think about you, but the positive far outweighs the negative.

Prayer

Lord, the thought of expressing my love for my friends isn't easy. But I do want to learn to love others the same way You love me. Help me, please.

Do not waste time bothering whether you "love" your neighbor. Act as if you did. As soon as we do this we find one of the great secrets. When you are behaving as if you love someone, you will presently come to love him.[5] —C.S. Lewis

JOURNAL
(QUIET TIME NOTES, PRAYER NEEDS, TODAY'S TO-DO'S)

| |
| |
| |
| |
| |
| |
| |
| |
| |

Today's Action

Read *John 15:13*. Talk with your prayer partners about how much you value your friends. See how you can encourage the others in your prayer group to choose whom they will serve.

Therefore, I need to. . .

I Hate It When I Do That!

The Big Idea

"I can't believe I said that!" I hate it when I do that!"

"How could I have let her talk me into this? I hate it when I do that!"

"No, no! Why can't I control my thoughts? I hate it when I do that!"

Each of us will "blow it" at times. It seems that when it happens, all the wrong people are around. Those people we want to be an example to, end up being the very people who are eyewitnesses of our blunders. Don't come down too hard on yourself, though.

> *"There is no one righteous, not even one"* (Rom. 3:10).

Nobody's perfect. And that includes you. It's inevitable that you're going to mess up. Don't think that you're alone.

Guilt from mistakes you've made can stop you in your tracks as you try to pray for your friends. Don't let anything stand in your way of seeing your friends come to Christ. Continually pattern your living after Jesus' example.

What's the Point?

Jesus is our model. Let's imitate Him. His Spirit in us gives us the ability to do so. Even in our imperfect way, let's keep on praying for our friends.

Think About It

Everybody messes up! You're going to also. Don't disqualify yourself because of a few mistakes.

Prayer

Lord, I know there's plenty of times that I've blown it. Thank You for forgiving me and giving me other chances to serve You.

IF, instead of fighting God or doubting Him in times of adversity, we will seek to cooperate with God, we will find that we will be drawn into a deeper relationship with Him.[6] —Jerry Bridges

JOURNAL
(QUIET TIME NOTES, PRAYER NEEDS, TODAY'S TO-DO'S)

Today's Action

Read *John 18:25*. Let your prayer partners know about an area where you've blown it. Pray about it with them. They may have some helpful suggestions, too!

Therefore, I need to. . .

Failure Is Never Permanent

The Big Idea

Hockey is an interesting game. The penalty system is especially intriguing. The referees watch all the players. Players with too many penalties are sent past the penalty box and to the locker-room for the rest of the game.

If we played the game of life like that, we would have penalties every day. Sometimes, we think that God is like a big referee in the sky. We imagine a cosmic locker-room where we'll be sent if we keep messing up and going against the rules.

Guess what? God doesn't work like that. In His rule book, failure is never permanent.

> *Everyone has sinned and is far away from God's saving presence. But by the free gift of God's grace all are put right with him through Christ Jesus, who sets them free* (Rom. 3:23-24, TEV).

What's the Point?

His forgiveness is available to everyone who asks for it. He knows that we can't measure up on our own. Try this: the next time you "fail," (1) admit to God that you've sinned, (2) accept Jesus' forgiveness, and (3) with God's help, plan not to sin in that way again.

Think About It

Failure is never permanent. God's forgiveness is always available. Just accept it.

Prayer

Father, I know that there are times I still struggle with sin. I am so thankful for my Christian friends who hold me accountable. Help me be honest with them about the area of my life where You want control.

> God is a god of grace. Salvation is His free gift. We can never earn it. Yet we still attempt to live the Christian life as though our salvation depended totally on our actions. We put ourselves under a burden of legalism.[7]—Jerry White

JOURNAL
(QUIET TIME NOTES, PRAYER NEEDS, TODAY'S TO-DO'S)

Today's Action

Read *Romans 8:6*. Don't think that because you sin, it's pointless to pray with your prayer partners. Each of us have areas of our life where God needs more control. Partner together with them to begin giving control of those areas to God. Pray with your prayer partners about the most significant area of your life where God wants control.

Therefore, I need to. . .

Under the Microscope

The Big Idea

There I was, standing among my friends with a beer can in my hand. I'll never forget the stinging words, "Oh, and YOU'RE supposed to be the big CHRISTIAN." What a painful lesson that was. The person who said that, had "talked" the Christian talk but wasn't "walking" the Christian walk. Was his credibility as a Christian totally ruined? Probably for the person who confronted him it was. Maybe not permanently, but he would have a long way to go before he could prove that his Christianity was real. God forgave him, and he was finally able to forgive himself, but it would probably be a long time before his life would matter to that person.

Once we say we belong to Christ we go under the microscope, and other people start watching.

> *I urge you to live a life worthy of the calling you have received (Eph. 4:1).*

What's the Point?

Ask yourself: Do I talk differently? Do I gossip, or tell the same jokes and stories as everyone else? Do I really live differently? Do I participate in the same activities that I did before Christ changed my life? What's different about me?

Think About It

If you talk the talk, you need to walk the walk. People are watching to see if what you have is for real.

Prayer

Lord, there's a lot of truth in the old saying, "If you talk the talk, you gotta walk the walk." I know that sometimes I'm not very consistent. Help me to be the real thing—all the time.

God created things that had free will...free will, though it makes evil possible, is also the only thing that makes possible any love or goodness or joy worth having.[8] —C. S. Lewis

JOURNAL
(QUIET TIME NOTES, PRAYER NEEDS, TODAY'S TO-DO'S)

Today's Action

Read *James 5:16*. In your prayer partnerships, continue confessing shortcomings you have in your own life. Let your prayer partners be honest with you about things that they see in your own life, too. Be open to their suggestions. Then spend some time praying about it.

Therefore, I need to. . .

Sweat It Out!

The Big Idea

Have you ever watched a sports team practice, and wondered why they do all those weird drills? If you haven't actually been on a team like that, it may look kind of silly. They go through all sorts of seemingly meaningless drills over and over. If you ask the players which part of practice was their favorite, they'd probably say, "The end!" If it's not fun or easy, why practice? Because they know practice helps them achieve their goal as an athlete.

Each of us puts a lot of effort into being good at certain things: we study for tests, memorize sports player's names and statistics, learn the words to our favorite songs. Sure, this effort is worth something, but wouldn't it be great if we put that same effort toward something that lasted longer than just this lifetime?

> *Keep yourself in training for a godly life. Physical exercise has some value, but spiritual exercise is valuable in every way, because it promises life both for the present and for the future* (1 Tim 4:7-8, TEV).

What's the Point?

The challenge is to train ourselves to be godly, even though we know it'll be hard. After all, the benefits are out of this world!

Think About It

Just like we spend many hours training for earthly activities, we must spend energy and time toward growing in godliness, no matter how tough it is.

Prayer

Father, I'm thankful for the opportunity to grow and mature and become more like You. Thank You for Your patience and willingness to mold me into Your likeness.

Go confidently in the direction of your dreams
and live the life you've imagined.[9] —Unknown

JOURNAL
(QUIET TIME NOTES, PRAYER NEEDS, TODAY'S TO-DO'S)

Today's Action

Read *1 Timothy 6:11*. Talk with your prayer partners this
week about one way you want to grow in godliness. Listen
to their suggestions too. Don't forget to ask each other
each week how you are doing in these areas.

Therefore, I need to. . .

If You Aim At Nothing, You'll Hit It Every Time

The Big Idea

When your family plans a trip, they have to know at least three things: where they're going, where they are now, and how they want to get there. They have a plan. Without a plan they might get lost or run around in circles.

It makes sense to have a plan. A house isn't built without a blue print. A product isn't sold without a marketing strategy. A war isn't won without a battle plan. Don't you think that we need a plan for living, too? This guy has a plan; a plan that got him where he wanted to go.

> Brothers, I do not consider myself yet to have taken hold of it. But one thing I do: Forgetting what is behind and straining toward what is ahead, I press on toward the goal to win the prize for which God has called me heavenward in Christ Jesus (Phil. 3:13-14).

What's the Point?

This week you've been shown a plan for living called "The Live the Life Challenge."

C ommit yourself to Christ

H onor Christ in your moral life

R espect authority

I nvolve yourself with other Christians

S eek God through prayer

T ake the message of Christ to my friends

Why not use this as your guide and take the challenge?

Think About It

Don't just "float" through the Christian life like a leaf on a stream, choose a path and take it!

Prayer

Father, I know there's plenty of times that I just wing it and hope for the best, even in my relationship with You. Help me to grow purposefully in my relationship with You.

My life and my ministry are intertwined, and the connecting thread is the time I spend alone with God.[10]—Steve Young

JOURNAL
(QUIET TIME NOTES, PRAYER NEEDS, TODAY'S TO-DO'S)

Today's Action

Read *Philippians 1:20*. Use the Live the Life Challenge as a checkpoint with your prayer partners. Talk about the one area where you are strongest. Then pick one area that's weak, tell each other about it, and plan to work on it this week.

Therefore, I need to. . .

The Cowardly Lion

The Big Idea

Well, the path is yellow and the castle is big. The journey has been long. The reward at the end is a heart, a brain, courage, and a way home. Each one of the characters has rehearsed what they would ask the Wizard. Yet when the time comes to ask, they are afraid and they run.

Just like the characters in the *Wizard of Oz*, we all have a little fear. Many of us fear telling others about Christ. The goal is to tell your story, not some plan or a set of verses that don't mean a lot to you. You get to tell your friends (with whom you have shared so many other things) about the One that never leaves you and always loves you no matter what.

> "Never will I leave you; never will I forsake you." So we say with confidence, "The Lord is my helper; I will not be afraid. What can man do to me?" (Heb. 13:5b-6).

What's the Point?

The promise is simple: God will never leave you or forsake you, and He is your helper. He is not some weird wizard behind a curtain pushing buttons and pulling levers. He is a personal, loving God that stays with you and helps you even when you are afraid.

Think About It

Your friends need to hear from a friend that God is personal and approachable and desires to build a relationship with them.

Prayer

Lord, because You saved me You gave me a story to tell. Help me have the courage to look for the opportunity, and share that story with my friends.

One day, while my son Zac and I were out in the country, climbing around in some cliffs, I heard a voice from above me yell, "Hey Dad! Catch me!" I turned around to see Zac joyfully jumping off a rock straight at me...I gasped, "Zac! Can you give me one good reason why you did that?" He responded with remarkable calmness.
"Sure...because you're my dad." His whole assurance was based on the fact that his father was trustworthy."—Tim Hansel

JOURNAL
(QUIET TIME NOTES, PRAYER NEEDS, TODAY'S TO-DO'S)

| |
| |
| |
| |
| |
| |
| |
| |

Today's Action

Read *Psalm 96:3*. Write what God has done for you personally. Ask Him to give you an opportunity to share that story with a friend.

Therefore, I need to. . .

The Courage of a Boy

The Big Idea

Fear gripped the young teenager. All he knew was that the giant before him was threatening to kill his family. For days, they had lived in fear for their lives. No one had the courage to face that monster of a man. Now, the boy stood in front of this huge man. If he lived in fear, his family and friends would die. He had a decision to make: live in fear, or have the courage to do something. The decision was made, David stood his ground, he faced the giant, and God delivered the giant into his hands.

> David said to the Philistine, "You come against me with sword and spear and javelin, but I come against you in the name of the Lord Almighty, the God of the armies of Israel, whom you have defied. This day the Lord will hand you over to me, and I'll strike you down and cut off your head" (1 Sam. 17:45-46).

What's the Point?

Our faith in God can overcome fear. God can give you courage.

Think About It

As you think about sharing your story with your friends, they may seem like giants, but they aren't. Even though we are fearful, we must overcome that fear with faith. And then, the Lord will use us.

Prayer

Lord, there are all kinds of Goliath's in my life that sometimes scare me...and the thought of sharing my faith can be one big Goliath. God, give me courage.

Everything as to what you become, and as to what you accomplish for the glory of God and His Kingdom depends upon prayer as it depends on nothing else in the entire world.[12]—Unknown

JOURNAL
(QUIET TIME NOTES, PRAYER NEEDS, TODAY'S TO-DO'S)

Today's Action

Read *1 Corinthians 16:13*. As you prepare to share your story with your friends, identify your fears and begin asking Christ to give you the courage to face and overcome your fears. Pray about this with your prayer partners.

Therefore, I need to. . .

The Fear of the Wolf

The Big Idea

It's simple. He had to decide. If he did not construct a sturdy house, the Big Bad Wolf was going to come and "huff and puff and blow his house down." The wolf had already gotten his two brothers' houses. They built them out of straw and sticks. They looked good, and could have won a blue ribbon for using recycled materials and being environmentally correct, but they did not keep the wolf out! Fear drove the third pig to build his house out of brick; a stronger material to hold out the wolf. For us, fear can also drive us to make better choices and to rely on something or someone who is stronger and greater than us.

> He said to me "My grace is sufficient for you, for my power is made perfect in weakness." Therefore I will boast all the more gladly about my weaknesses, so that Christ's power may rest on me (2 Cor. 12:9).

What's the Point?

As you begin sharing your story with your friends, Christ wants you to admit your fears and weaknesses, so that He can work through you.

Think About It

God knows your strengths and your weaknesses. And His power is at work in you. Don't rely on your strengths or weaknesses. Rely on His power.

Prayer

Lord, I know that You know my strengths and weaknesses intimately. I know that You can both increase my strength and lessen my weaknesses. Thank You for working in my life.

You can simply refuse to doubt. You can shut the door against every suggestion of doubt that comes, and you can by faith declare exactly the opposite.[13]—Hanna Whitall Smith

JOURNAL
(QUIET TIME NOTES, PRAYER NEEDS, TODAY'S TO-DO'S)

| |
| |
| |
| |
| |
| |
| |
| |

Today's Action

Read *Acts 4:29*. This week, pray about your story and the fact that you'll share it with your friends. Speak boldly, not out of fear, but out of the power of Christ.

Therefore, I need to. . .

Supper for the Lions

The Big Idea

As a young man, he kneeled in a small room praying. He knew that if he got caught it would cost him his life. The law said that you were not to worship God. So, in the privacy of his room, he prayed. He had made up his mind years before that he would not give in or allow fear of death to cause him to abandon God. The time on his knees cost him indeed. He was thrown into a pit full of lions. There was something about Daniel that allowed his faith to overcome any fear of people or circumstances.

In *Daniel 6:10-11*, we see Daniel's reaction when the King gave the order for him not to pray to anyone but the king.

> *Now when Daniel learned the the decree had been published, he went home to his upstairs room where the windows opened toward Jerusalem. Three times a day he got down on his knees and prayed, giving thanks to his God, just as he had done before (Dan. 6:10-11).*

What's the Point?

For you to have a faith that will help you overcome any fear of sharing your story, there must be a deep conviction and confidence that God will protect you.

Think About It

Is God big enough to take care of your fears? You might face rejection or someone making fun of you, or labeling you a "Jesus freak," but you are not facing death or a lions den. God wants you to be assured that He can give you the faith to overcome any fear you might have. Are you ready?

Prayer

God, I'm ready! You have given me faith and encouraged me by the example of Daniel. Help me to be an overcomer!

He may hide Himself from our sense of His presence, but He never allows our adversaries to hide us from Him. He may allow us to pass through the deep waters and the fire, but He will be with us in them.[14]—Jerry Bridges

JOURNAL
(QUIET TIME NOTES, PRAYER NEEDS, TODAY'S TO-DO'S)

Today's Action

Read *John 20:21*. Daniel took a risk and was a pacesetter. God is asking you to take a risk for your friends who need to hear what Jesus has done in your life.

Therefore, I need to. . .

In Disguise

The Big Idea

For years he had hidden his identity. Surely there was some speculation and suspicion among the people. His parents knew, but no one else did. When he fell in love, even his girlfriend didn't know for a long time. Was he ashamed of his true self, or just afraid of what others might think? Well, you and I think of him as Superman and the mild-mannered newspaper reporter Clark Kent, the ever-bungling klutz. Like Clark, many of us hide who we really are. We are the mild-mannered Christian at home and sometimes at church. But we have never revealed to our friends that we belong to Jesus. Our friends need to know our true identity.

> *"Whoever acknowledges me before men, I will also acknowledge him before my Father in heaven. But whoever disowns me before men, I will disown him before my Father in heaven"* (Matt. 10:32-33).

What's the Point?

Sounds tough and hard. Yet we are in a serious war; a war where the stakes are high. The stakes are the eternal lives of your friends.

Think About It

God does not need you to be Superman or Clark Kent. He wants you to be who you really are: a person with a story of Jesus working in your life. Your friends need to hear that story.

Prayer

Father, I know that I am a work in progress. I know that I belong to You, and for that I'm thankful. Help me to be honest and real in front of my friends, even in my struggles.

Let the world know you as you are, not as you think you should be, because sooner or later, if you are posing, you will forget the pose, and then where are you?[15]—Unknown

JOURNAL
(QUIET TIME NOTES, PRAYER NEEDS, TODAY'S TO-DO'S)

| |
| |
| |
| |
| |
| |
| |
| |

Today's Action

Read *Ephesians 4:22-24*. Do your friends see you as having two different personalities? It's time to reveal who you really are. Ask God for faith and courage to take a stand on your true identity. If you've played both sides, ask Christ to give you the strength to be honest and open to your friends. Then ask Jesus to help you be who you really are!

Therefore, I need to. . .

Decisions Along the Way

The Big Idea

It is time to eat. You are in a car full of friends. Someone asks, "Where should we eat?" The debate is on. In the end the choice is made. You choose the "Arches," not the "Bell," the "Colonel," or the "Hut."

Driving to your chosen destination often means driving right past the other destinations. In the end, one choice is made to the exclusion of others. Saying yes to one destination means saying no to others.

When you placed your faith in Christ as your Savior you said: "Yes; I will follow You." That decision means you say no to all other destinations.

> As Jesus was walking beside the Sea of Galilee, he saw two brothers, Simon called Peter and his brother Andrew. They were casting a net into the lake, for they were fishermen . "Come, follow me," Jesus said, "and I will make you fishers of men." At once they left their nets and followed him (Matt. 4:18-20).

What's the Point?

Peter and Andrew lived with the reality that saying, "Yes, I will follow," required leaving their nets.

Think About It

Throughout your journey of faith you will have to make difficult decisions. Your non-Christian friends see and respect these decisions. Choose wisely everyday.

Prayer

Lord, just for today, help me to make smart decisions. I understand that sometimes smart decisions aren't necessarily the easy ones. Help me to stay clear-headed and to listen for Your directions.

I was a prisoner to my feelings, I mistakenly thought I could not trust God unless I felt like trusting Him...Now I am learning that trusting God is first of all a matter of the will, and is not dependent on my feelings. I choose to trust God and my feelings eventually follow.[16]—Jerry Bridges

JOURNAL
(QUIET TIME NOTES, PRAYER NEEDS, TODAY'S TO-DO'S)

| |
| |
| |
| |
| |
| |
| |

Today's Action

Reread *Matthew 4:18-20*. Your prayer partners struggle with these decisions every day just like you do. *An Awesome Way to Pray* is undoubtedly requiring you to make some tough decisions. Talk with your prayer partners about your struggles to "Leave your nets and follow." Together you can support each other.

Therefore, I need to. . .

Your Journey Is Unique

The Big Idea

Giant cruise ships take people from one port to another every day. On board, people can choose to swim, eat, jog, eat, sunbathe, eat , play basketball, eat, shop, eat, dance, or eat. Hundreds of people travel to the same destination; however, each journey is unique. The uniqueness of each journey depends on the choices, tastes, and talents of the traveler.

Your journey of faith may be a bit like taking a cruise. In the end, we are headed toward eternity; our destination established. Our choices today determine our experience on the journey.

> *You cannot fool God, so don't make a fool of yourself! You will harvest what you plant. If you follow your selfish desires, you will harvest destruction, but if your follow the Spirit, you will harvest eternal life. Don't get tired of helping others. You will be rewarded when the time is right , if you don't give up* (Gal. 6:7-9, CEV).

What's the Point?

Our choices have a powerful impact on our lives, both negatively and positively.

Think About It

As a Christian, God has allowed you the responsibility of making choices. You can use those choices positively or negatively. Choose carefully.

Prayer

Lord, I can see that so much of my life is decided by the choices that I make. I know my destination is with You; just help me make the right choices as I make the journey!

God's justice is never divorced from His right-eousness. He never condemns the innocent. He never clears the guilty. He never punishes with undo severity. He never fails to reward righteous-ness. His justice is perfect justice.[17]—R. C. Sproul

JOURNAL
(QUIET TIME NOTES, PRAYER NEEDS, TODAY'S TO-DO'S)

Today's Action

Read *Joshua 24:15*. Your life is greatly affected by the choices you make. Consider one good choice and one bad choice you've made recently. What impact did these choices have? Share this with your prayer partners this week.

Therefore, I need to. . .

Storms Happen

The Big Idea

Ferries make trips across the English Channel many times a day, all year round. Recently, one of these ferries traveled across the English Channel carrying people and cars. Some people settled in to eat and talk during the journey. Others just stayed in their cars and slept. In the beginning, this trip looked just like the many trips completed on previous days. But a storm came. The ship's enormous doors burst open during the storm, and the ship sank in less than five minutes!

You will have storms that test your faith. It is during tough times that our faith is either destroyed or deepened.

> *Trust in the Lord with all your heart and lean not on your own understanding; in all your ways acknowledge him, and he will make your paths straight (Prov. 3:5-6).*

What's the Point?

Storms, tough times, will come; during these storms that test your faith, who do you plan to trust?

Think About It

The evidence that you are linked with God is not the presence or absence of storms, but how you respond. Do not allow tough times to destroy your faith. Trust in the Lord with all your heart and ask Him to deepen your faith.

Prayer

Father, I know that tough times will come in life. I know, too, that although You don't necessarily remove the storms, You are always with me through the storms. Thank You!

> God is the supreme judge of the universe...There is no corruption in Him. No one can bribe Him. He refuses to show partiality. He is no respecter of persons. He never acts out of ignorance. He does not make mistakes.[18]—A.W. Tozer

JOURNAL
(QUIET TIME NOTES, PRAYER NEEDS, TODAY'S TO-DO'S)

| |
| |
| |
| |
| |
| |
| |
| |
| |

Today's Action

Read *John 14:1*. We don't understand everything about God's plan (if we could, we'd be God, right?). Take time when storms are absent to prepare for the future storms. What is one small thing you can trust God for that will build your faith? Share this with your prayer partners.

Therefore, I need to. . .

Others on the Journey

The Big Idea

One of the most enjoyable aspects of traveling is having friends along to enjoy the trip. You have met and prayed with a few friends for the past several weeks. You may know many others who have been involved with prayer partnerships as well.

Million of others are on the same journey you are on. All across the world while you are reading these words, Christians from every race are praying, worshiping, fasting, suffering, witnessing, and learning.

> God did not appoint us to suffer wrath, but to receive salvation through our Lord Jesus Christ. Therefore encourage one another and build each other up, just as in fact you are doing (1 Thess. 5:9,11).

What's the Point?

You are not on this journey alone! Your partnership in the gospel with others throughout the world should encourage you. You may never meet a Japanese or Slovakian Christian, but every day you meet with your friends who are Christians. You can encourage them!

Think About It

Do you ever get discouraged as a Christian? You are not alone. Your friends struggle with their feelings just like you do. You can build up your faith by encouraging others in their faith.

Prayer

There are times, Lord, when I feel like I'm the only person who is going through all these trials and temptations. But I know I'm not alone. Help me to be an encouragement to someone else.

> There are many things you can do in your life without faith. Without faith you can get married. Without faith you can have a home. Without faith you can become a millionaire. Without faith you can live a normal, relatively happy life. But there's one thing you cannot do without faith. "Without faith it is impossible to please God."[19]
> —Walter A. Henrichsen

JOURNAL
(QUIET TIME NOTES, PRAYER NEEDS, TODAY'S TO-DO'S)

Today's Action

Read *Hebrews 3:13*. Think about the other students and leaders involved in *An Awesome Way to Pray*. Choose one or two to purposely encourage in their faith this week.

Therefore, I need to. . .

Friends Are Watching

The Big Idea

Teenagers are almost legendary for making crazy choices.
You may be able to list a few things you have done that
were not the best decisions in the world. We all have times
in our lives that are like scenes from *Dumb and Dumber*.
At the height of your "dumbness" somebody probably
asked, "What kind of example are you?" One of the hardest
things to do is to be a good example.

> *Don't let anyone look down on you because you are young, but set an
> example for the believers in speech, in life, in love, in faith, and in purity.
> Be diligent in these matters; give yourself wholly to them, so that everyone
> may see your progress* (1 Tim. 4:12, 15).

What's the Point?

Put your faith into action in all areas of your life so other
Christians can see and be encouraged.

Think About It

Getting your beliefs and actions to match up is difficult.
That must be why we are told to "give ourselves wholly" to
this problem. Nothing less than a whole-hearted obedience
will make up good examples to our friends.

Prayer

Lord, help me to be faithful in all my actions, because I
know that people are watching. Help me to model Your life
in me.

Nothing honors God like praising Him for what He promised before the promise is fulfilled. That is the ultimate expression of faith.[20]
—Charles Stanley

JOURNAL
(QUIET TIME NOTES, PRAYER NEEDS, TODAY'S TO-DO'S)

Today's Action

Read *Titus* 2:7. Is there anyone you need to go to and ask forgiveness for setting a bad example? Go to them this week.

Therefore, I need to. . .

Mission Impossible!

The Big Idea

Have you ever made a New Year's Resolution—decided to turn over a new leaf—then, after only a week, or a day, or maybe even an hour, you've already blown it? It's no different in the Christian life when we try to live up to rules we've made for ourselves. In fact, Paul apparently had the same problem.

> I don't do the good I want to do; instead, I do the evil that I do not want to do (Rom. 7:19, TEV).

What's the Point?

The good news is that even though we can't live the Christian life in our own strength, we can live it through the power of God's Spirit who lives in us. We can "try and try" to live for Christ, but the secret is to "trust and trust" instead.

Think About It

You can't live the Christian life in your own strength. You have to depend on God's Spirit in you to live the Christian life through you.

Prayer

God, I know that You didn't make us to try to go it alone. Thank You for the presence and comfort of Your Spirit. Help me to trust You completely.

To know God's will, we must totally surrender to God's will. Our tendency is to make God's decision for him...Don't go to God with options and expect Him to choose one of your preferences. Go to Him with empty hands—no hidden agendas, no crossed fingers, nothing behind your back. Go to him with a willingness to do whatever he says.[21] —Max Lucado

JOURNAL
(QUIET TIME NOTES, PRAYER NEEDS, TODAY'S TO-DO'S)

| |
| |
| |
| |
| |
| |
| |
| |
| |

Today's Action

Read 2 *Thessalonians 2:16-17*. Pray with your prayer partners about living the Christian life with God's strength instead of your own. Encourage them to rely on Him too.

Therefore, I need to. . .

House Guest...Christ Lives in Us

The Big Idea

"Company's coming...clean up your room!" Sound familiar? When company was coming to my house, there would be a wild cleaning frenzy, and everyone had to do their part. Sometimes, just to finish quicker, I'd hide things in the closet, under the bed, in a drawer. Presto! The room was clean—as long as nobody looked too closely!

Often we do this in our relationship with Jesus, too. We ask Him to come into our lives, but we try to hide the things we think He doesn't want to see...you know, those sins we have that we don't want Him to know about. But the truth is, when we ask Christ to come into our lives, He comes in to every part of our lives.

> *God demonstrates his own love for us in this: While we were still sinners, Christ died for us (Rom. 5:8).*

What's the Point?

You see? He already knows about the things we try to hide; He knew about it when He died for us. He wants to clean out all the "junk" in our lives. We just need to allow Him to do it.

Think About It

Don't try to hide those "secret sins" from God. He knows already; just admit to Him that they're there. He'll help you overcome those problems too!

Prayer

Lord, I know that You're aware of my secret sins. My life is an open book before You. Help me to honestly confront those secret areas, and offer them to You freely and without fear.

Ultimately, God will allow nothing to escape;
every detail of our lives is under His scrutiny.[22]
—Oswald Chambers

JOURNAL
(QUIET TIME NOTES, PRAYER NEEDS, TODAY'S TO-DO'S)

Today's Action

Read *Proverbs 15:31-32*. Confessing those sins you've hidden for so long is the first step toward changing them. Who knows? Your prayer partners may have struggled with some of the same problems and have some answers for you. Confess your sins to each other this week.

Therefore, I need to. . .

Can You Do a One-Eighty?

The Big Idea

I've always enjoyed action adventure movies, especially the car chase scenes. You've seen it when an actor is going in one direction, but then, all of a sudden, he cuts the wheels hard to the left, slams on the brakes, and spins around. In the end he's facing in the exact opposite direction. He's turned the car around a complete 180 degrees. He did a one-eighty.

> *Flee the evil desires of youth, and pursue righteousness, faith, love and peace, along with those who call on the Lord out of a pure heart* (2 Tim. 2:22).

What's the Point?

Picture yourself in a car chase scene. You're speeding down the street heading right toward *the evil desires of youth*. This verse is saying that you need to "do a one-eighty!" You need to turn around completely and go in the opposite direction.

We do this when we first come to Christ. The Bible calls it *repentance*. We turn away from the things we were doing, and turn toward Jesus and His ways. Repentance is not only something we do when we become Christians. It is the lifestyle of a Christian.

Think About It

All through our Christian lives, there will be circumstances that we need to "run away from" or "flee."

Prayer

Thank You, Father, for making me aware of the times that I need to repent of sin. Help me move from awareness to true repentance and turn away from the things that dishonor You.

Once you decide you want to do God's will, there will be some fears, because we're generally afraid to commit ourselves to Him. We tend to think, Man, if I tell God I'll do anything, He'll send me out to be a little, green, shriveled-up missionary in Africa. But if God would want you to do that, you'll be happiest in that situation because His will is good, pleasing, and perfect.[23]
—Russ Johnson

JOURNAL
(QUIET TIME NOTES, PRAYER NEEDS, TODAY'S TO-DO'S)

| |
| |
| |
| |
| |
| |
| |

Today's Action

Read *Matthew 6:33*. Encourage your prayer partners to *pursue righteousness*. Let them know that you're committed to them for the long haul, not just for this six weeks.

Therefore, I need to. . .

Christianity: A Team Sport

The Big Idea

I'm amazed by the teamwork on a soccer team. Each person is working toward the same goal. Each player knows that he alone cannot achieve the goal; they have to help each other or they will lose.

Yesterday we talked about running away from evil desires of youth. That's only half the plan. Rather than just running away and reacting to the situations around us, we need to plan the direction. Let's look at the verse again.

> Flee the evil desires of youth, and pursue righteousness, faith, love and peace, along with those who call on the Lord out of a pure heart (2 Tim. 2:22).

What's the Point?

So, the Bible says to turn from evil and pursue those other godly things. We need to run purposefully toward Jesus and the things that He desires for us to have: righteousness, faith, love, and peace.

Now, look at the last part of the verse again. It says that we're not to do this by ourselves like that old black-and-white TV hero, The Lone Ranger. We are to seek out others who call on the Lord out of a pure heart. We need each other to achieve the goal of righteousness, faith, and all the rest. It helps us when we help each other.

Think About It

You cannot live the Christian life alone; it requires a team effort.

Prayer

Thank You, Lord, for my Christian friends. I don't know what I'd do without the encouragement they give me.

The will of God is far more like a scroll that unrolls every day. In other words, God has a will for you and me today and tomorrow and the next day and the day after that...It is not something to be grasped as a package once for all.[24]
—Paul E. Little

JOURNAL
(QUIET TIME NOTES, PRAYER NEEDS, TODAY'S TO-DO'S)

Today's Action

Read *Matthew 5:6*. Ask your prayer partners to encourage you to *pursue righteousness*. Let them know that you're committed to them for the long haul, not just for this six weeks.

Therefore, I need to. . .

Follow the Leader

The Big Idea

I looked across the field and saw my bird dog, Gypsy, playing a "follow the leader" game with her puppies. She would dart left, then right, then make a big circle, and obediently her pups would all follow behind her in a straight line. It was funny to watch them, but for Gypsy, it was more than just a game. She was training them to be good hunters. She knew these movements would help them develop the keen senses required of a bird dog. She was their teacher and their example.

As Christians, we have a teacher and example as well. Jesus told His disciples to follow Him, and as they did, He showed them how they were to live. They went where He went, ate what He ate, slept where He slept, and did what He did.

This is how we know we are in him: Whoever claims to live in him must walk as Jesus did (1 John 2:5b-6).

What's the Point?

Even though Jesus isn't physically with us, we have His example in Christian leaders, the Bible, and the Holy Spirit in us. As we "follow the leader" we become leaders ourselves to newer and younger Christians. Are you ready to become the leader?

Think About It

Christ has given us the responsibility to both follow Him, and lead others. Are you willing to take both responsibilities?

Prayer

Lord, there are so many in my life worthy of imitating. Help me to be that kind of encouragement for someone else.

If you picture Time as a straight line along which we have to travel, then you must picture God as the whole page on which the line is drawn. We come to the parts of the line one by one: we have to leave A behind before we get to B, and cannot reach C until we leave B behind. God, from above or outside or all around, contains the whole line and sees it all.[25] —C.S. Lewis

JOURNAL
(QUIET TIME NOTES, PRAYER NEEDS, TODAY'S TO-DO'S)

Today's Action

Read *1 Corinthians 15:58*. This week ask your prayer partners to pray that you will be leaders.

Therefore, I need to...

The Never-Ending Struggle

The Big Idea
Have you ever wanted to trade in part of your physical
body? We all have things about our bodies we would like to
change—hair, figure, pimples, big feet, fat, weird ears, etc.
Often we want to change our circumstances too. Actually
there are lots of physical and circumstantial things in our
lives that are a constant pain. Paul knew that also.

> To keep me from becoming conceited because of these surpassingly great rev-
> elations, there was given me a thorn in my flesh, a messenger of Satan, to
> torment me. Three times I pleaded with the Lord to take it away from me.
> But he said to me, "My grace is sufficient for you, for my power is made
> perfect in weakness." Therefore I will boast all the more gladly about my
> weaknesses, so that Christ's power may rest on me. That is why, for
> Christ's sake, I delight in weaknesses, in insults, in hardships, in persecu-
> tions, in difficulties. For when I am weak, then I am strong (2 Cor. 12:7-
> 10).

What's the Point?
Because of your thorn or flaw, you can be stronger in your
walk and witness for Christ.

Think About It
We don't know what the thorn was in Paul's life, yet we do
know that it caused him to depend on Christ more.
Because of his thorn or flaw, Paul was stronger in his walk
and witness for Christ. Your thorns will make you stronger!

Prayer
Father, it's hard for me to imagine what good can come out
of struggles and hardships, and it's even harder to imagine
why You might allow me to be persecuted. But I'm confi-
dent that You're always protecting me and growing me.

Don't doubt in the darkness what God has shown you in the light.[26]—Unknown

JOURNAL
(QUIET TIME NOTES, PRAYER NEEDS, TODAY'S TO-DO'S)

| |
| |
| |
| |
| |
| |
| |
| |
| |

Today's Action

Read *Ephesians 6:12*. As you think about living out your faith to your friends and telling your story, what "thorns" make it hard for you to do that?

Therefore, I need to. . .

The Never-Ending Thrill

The Big Idea

The cliff, known as "Big Bubba," is 150 feet tall. It's a 150 foot free rappel. When you step off the ledge at the top, there is no turning back. The only way out is down. You hang in midair; your only source of safety and security is the rope that is sliding through your figure eight. You have committed to do this; you want to do it. You trust your instructors and teachers; you have watched others do it safely and they lived to tell about it. You are sure you will be the first person to die, but you go for it anyway.

Over the past six weeks you have taken some risks with your non-Christian friends. You have shared your story. You have lived through it. What's next?

Jesus took risks too. For one, He was called a "friend of sinners."

"The Son of Man came eating and drinking, and you say, 'Here is a glutton and a drunkard, a friend of tax collectors and "sinners"'" (Luke 7:34).

What's the Point?

To be a true friend may require you to take some risks, using Jesus Christ as your example.

Think About It

Do the friends with whom you've been sharing your story see themselves as a religious project that you must endure, or do they see you as a true friend? Do you love them even though you do not like the sin in their lives?

Prayer

It's always kind of tricky, Lord, to be a friend to those who don't know You without getting involved in what they do. Help me to love my friends with Your kind of love and protect me from temptation.

What matters most in life is not what ladders we climb or what ownings we accumulate. What matters most is a relationship.[27]—Max Lucado

JOURNAL
(QUIET TIME NOTES, PRAYER NEEDS, TODAY'S TO-DO'S)

| |
| |
| |
| |
| |
| |
| |
| |

Today's Action

Read *Philippians 4:6*. Throughout the school year, you are going to have to take a risk by continuing the friendship even though your non-Christian friends might not commit to Christ. You have stepped off the cliff, the only way to finish is to see the friendship through until they come to Christ. Keep praying and being a friend.

Therefore, I need to. . .

The Never-Ending Ride

The Big Idea

What if you could get on your favorite roller coaster with your best friend and ride as long as you wanted? Wow! You and your friend would never forget such an incredible experience.

Praying with your friend bonds you together like that. You share your heart, laugh, and cry. And Jesus is with you all the way!

> *"For where two or three come together in my name, there am I with them"* (Matt. 18:20).

What's the Point?

You've already experienced what a great ride this has been over the last few weeks. Keep riding!

Think About It

As you have prayed together over the last several weeks, Jesus has been with you. He was the unseen partner in your prayer group. With your prayer partners you have met with Jesus and bonded in your relationships.

Prayer

Lord, thank You for all that I've experienced with my friends over the last few weeks. I know You have a lot more in store for us. Help us to continue the journey in You.

God is not stingy, possessive, or materialistic. We often use people as things; He uses things to bless people. And He manifests His generosity through more important gifts than just material goods. He freely gives us the priceless intangibles of forgiveness, mercy, and love.[28]—Floyd McClung, Jr.

JOURNAL
(QUIET TIME NOTES, PRAYER NEEDS, TODAY'S TO-DO'S)

| |
| |
| |
| |
| |
| |
| |
| |

Today's Action

Reread *Matthew 18:20*. The relationship you have made with your prayer partners can continue. For you to be effective in your walk with Christ throughout the coming school years, these relationships and others like them must be a part of your Christian life. Just think about meeting with Jesus and your friends on a weekly basis; what an awesome ride!

Therefore, I need to. . .

The Never-Ending Journey

The Big Idea

Sixty-three miles in five days; what a trip! Three mountain tops, four rivers, the rain, the bus, the snakes. No shower or bath for the last three days. The packs felt more like a hundred pounds instead of fifty. It wasn't easy.

The guides said to pick a tree every hundred yards and then move to the next tree; those were our "faith trees." Each one represented another stop in the right direction. it wasn't long before the students realized they had more strength and stamina than they thought!

> *I know what it is to be in need, and I know what it is to have plenty. I have learned the secret of being content in any and every situation, whether well fed or hungry, whether living in plenty or in want. I can do everything through him who gives me strength (Phil. 4:12-13).*

What's the Point?

The Lord has given us the strength for our walk with Him.

Think About It

God wants us to keep on going from one "faith tree" to the next. You can do it through His strength.

Prayer

I'm beginning to realize, Lord, that this walk with You is a never-ending journey. I wouldn't change it for anything in the world. Thanks for an amazing adventure!

Life, people, circumstances will press on us what seems to be evil, but God will use it for good to bring us closer to His dream for us.[29]
—Lloyd John Ogilvie

JOURNAL
(QUIET TIME NOTES, PRAYER NEEDS, TODAY'S TO-DO'S)

| |
| |
| |
| |
| |
| |
| |
| |

Today's Action

Read *Philippians 3:12-14*. If you want to continue the journey with Christ, you must be willing to take the next step out of your spiritual comfort zone. Why stay at home and watch TV when you can climb faith-growing, prayer-deepening, gospel-sharing mountains? Determine to press on!

Therefore, I need to. . .

The Never-Ending Riddle

The Big Idea

"Pete and Repeat are sitting on a log, Pete falls off, who's left?" "Repeat."

"Pete and Repeat are sitting on a log, Pete falls off, who's left?" "Repeat."

"Pete and Repeat are sitting on a log, Pete falls off, who's left?" "Repeat."

When you were younger, didn't you get tired of this kind of riddle? They go on and on and on. Sometimes we feel the Christian walk can be that way. A never-ending riddle that goes on and on. Our walk with Christ is not a silly riddle; it is a process that allows Christ to work in our lives. Christ wants to mold us and make us more like Him.

> *Being confident of this, that he who began a good work in you will carry it on to completion until the day of Christ Jesus (Phil. 1:6).*

What's the Point?

To continue the journey with Christ, you must commit to press on.

Think About It

Are you willing to allow Christ to keep on working in you? He has begun the work, and wants to continue it.

Prayer

Lord, thank You for helping me stay faithful and consistent over the last few weeks. I pray that I've developed some habits that will continue to help me become more like You. Thanks for giving me the opportunity to follow You.

Since God has assured us that it is His will that all men be saved, we therefore know that when we pray for the salvation of anyone who has not crossed the deadline of final and permanent impenitence, we are praying according to His will.[30]—Paul R. Billheimer

JOURNAL
(QUIET TIME NOTES, PRAYER NEEDS, TODAY'S TO-DO'S)

Today's Action

Read *Philippians 1:6*. Our walk with Christ is a process. We couldn't handle it if God caused all the growth He has for us to happen in one day or week. It would be too painful. He works through a process. You should be stronger in your Christian walk than you were six weeks ago. Six weeks from now you will be even stronger. Allow God to keep working to make you who He wants you to be.

Therefore, I need to. . .

Where Do We Go From Here?

Congratulations! You did it. You may have seen victories and disappointments, but you've stayed the course. Now what? Follow these suggestions:

- Continue making the three friends...three times a week...praying for three non-Christian friends a priority.
- Continue with your daily quiet time.
- Join a Christian club on your campus. If there's not one, start one. (Your youth leader can help.)
- Take advantage of all student ministries at your church.
- Pray a half-day with your friends for continued vision.
- Never, ever give up! You may get discouraged sometimes, but hang in there. Allow God to strengthen your faith.

Keep on praying! That's the most important thing you can do to grow in Christ, move toward maturity, and impact your friends, your school, and your world for Christ.

Notes to Pages 21-79.1. Unknown. 2. DeHann, Dan *The God You Can Know* (Chicago: Moody Press, 1982) 43. 3. Tozer, A.W. *The Knowledge of the Holy* (San Francisco: Harper and Row, Pub. 1961) 8. 4. Morgan, G. Campbell *Hosea, The Heart and Holiness of God* (London: Marshall Morgan & Scott LTD, 1960) 19. 5. Lewis, C.S. *Mere Christianity* (New York: Macmillan Pub. Co., 1943, 1945, 1952) 101. 6. Bridges, Jerry *Trusting God* (Colorado Springs, CO: Navpress, 1988, 1993) 192. 7. White, Jerry *Honesty, Morality, and Conscience* (Colorado Springs, CO: Navpress, 1978) 175. 8. Lewis, C.S. *Mere Christianity* (New York: Macmillan Pub. Co., 1943, 1945, 1952) 110. 9. Unknown. 10. Young, Steve. Reach Out Youth Solutions, Norcross, GA. 11. Hansel, Tim *Holy Sweat* (Dallas: Word Pub., 1987) 46-47. 12. Unknown. 13. Smith, Hanna Whitall *The God of All Comfort* (New York: Ballantine Books, 1986) 130-131. 14. Bridges, Jerry *Trusting God* (Colorado Springs, CO: Navpress, 1988, 1993) 199. 15. Unknown. 16. Bridges, Jerry, *Trusting God*, 195. 17. Sproul, R.C. *The Holiness of God* (Wheaton, Ill: Tyndale House Pub., 1985) 143. 18. Tozer, A.W. *The Knowledge of the Holy*, 143. 19. Henrichsen, W.A. *Many Aspire, Few Attain* (Colorado Springs, CO: Navpress) 19. 20. Stanley, Charles *The Wonderful Spirit Filled Life* (Nashville: Thomas Nelson, 1992) 150. 21 Lucado, Max *On the Anvil* (Tyndale House Pub., 1985) 95-96. 22. Chambers, Oswald *My Utmost for His Highest:a special updated edition* (Oswald Chambers Pub. Assoc. Ltd., 1995) July 31. 23. Johnson, Russ *How to Know the Will of God* (Colorado Springs, CO: Navpress, 1976, 1981) 112. 24. Little, Paul E. *Affirming the Will of God* (Downers Grove, Ill: InterVarsity Press, 1971) 137. 25. Lewis, C.S. *Mere Christianity*, 132. 26 Unknown. 27. Lucado, Max *On the Anvil*, 71.27. McClung, Floyd, Jr. *The Father Heart of God* (Eugene, OR:Harvest House Pub. 1985) 28. 29. Ogilvie, Lloyd John *Lord of the Impossible* (Nashville: Abingdon Press, 1984) 54. Billheimer, Paul E. *Destined for the Throne* (Fort Washington, PENN: Christian Literature Crusade, 1975) 63.